EARTH IS MY CHURCH

EARTH IS MY CHURCH

Poems by
Eric Scott Sutherland

Accents Publishing • Lexington, Kentucky • 2020

Copyright © 2020 by Eric Scott Sutherland
All rights reserved

Printed in the United States of America

Accents Publishing
Editor: Katerina Stoykova
Cover Illustration: *Through the Ferns,* Cricket Press (Brian and Sara Turner)

Library of Congress Control Number: 2019957655
ISBN: 978-1-936628-54-4
First Edition

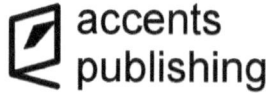

Accents Publishing is an independent press for brilliant voices. For a catalog of current and upcoming titles, please visit us on the Web at

www.accents-publishing.com

CONTENTS

An Idealist Ponders Extinction / 3
In the Medicine Bag / 5
Gorge / 6
Proof / 8
Earth Evolving Flower / 9
Light Now Like Feather / 10
Mitakuye Oyasin / 11
Becoming a Man / 13
Becoming Vegetarian / 14
A Native Speaks from the Grave / 18
Fractured Appalachia / 20
The Watchman / 23
Old Frankfort Pike Is a Spine of Mine / 24
Survival Mechanism / 27
Lifeboat / 28
The Tide / 30
Kentucky Is My Body / 31
Reclamation / 33
Turtle Slow / 35
Cone of Juvenility / 36
Microcosm / 37
How to Restore a Forest / 38
Biomimicry / 39
Religiosa / 40
Suns and Moons / 41
Off the Wagon Outside Waddy / 43
Savior / 44
Spiders / 45
The Center / 46
Good Mud / 47
Allegiance / 48
Mudroom Catharsis / 49
Instructions / 50
New Fire / 51
Great Spirit Apprentice / 52

Nothing Lasts Forever / 53
Ruin / 54
Disappear / 55
Earth Is My Church / 56
Pine Mountain: A Work in Progress / 58

About the Author / 63

Acknowledgments / 65

> There are no unsacred places;
> there are only sacred places
> and desecrated places.
>
> —Wendell Berry

> Humans are vulnerable and rely on the kindnesses of the earth and the sun;
> we exist together in a sacred field of meaning.
>
> —Joy Harjo

AN IDEALIST PONDERS EXTINCTION

If not hope
then what?

Widening disaster
threatens to waste
me
as it will
surely waste
all
the world.

Hope is
a torch
held aloft
in a monsoon
protected or doused
depending on
the will
of those carrying
the light.

Hope is
a tether
at this crossroad
abyss where
we choose
to hold
the lifeline
or ignore
and let loose.

Modern men
and women

both heroes
and fools; mastodons
in the final moments
before a world
of ice descends

enjoying the taste
of fresh buttercups.

IN THE MEDICINE BAG

a red-tailed hawk,
an eagle, a pelican
sitting inside a dream-
            catcher,
a turtle's femur,
a glistening crystal,
and two flesh pink stones
shaped like hearts.

GORGE

> "Silence is the language of God, all else is poor translation."
> —Rumi, as quoted in *Teachers of Wisdom* by Igor Kononenko

Vulpes vulpes leaves
feces and footsteps
behind
in the quiet of winter
        snow

Cliff top scalp
burned and bark
blackened from too
few rain drops last
        summer

Hiking Red River
Gorge engaged
in divine dialogue
that exists only in
        silence

Sources of light
saturating to blindness
weathered etchings
and yesterday's world
        exposed

In towering rock
shelters we step
through arches of time
following where wild ones
        walk

Touching echoes
there is no need to talk
Sunday morning
and nothing is more
        sacred

PROOF

of peace.

Copperhead sleeps
in cool shade

as I pluck blackberries
from thorny vines
and place them between my lips.

A dragonfly watches
from my shoulder.

The sky is a mist of humid
July air
droops heavy
toward the ground
everywhere my eyes
gaze upon the horizon.

And though I struggle
bent over like a seed head nodding
barehanded to move soil
enclosed in a liquid skin of sweat

I am as sure as my heart screams it.

EARTH EVOLVING FLOWER

Blue heron skies wheel
above lush Elkhorn
valley where Walt
Whitman still walks
through leaves of
bluegrass, Kentucky
River flyway some
sort of highway
for traveling birds.

I sit still, humming
my own winged song,
extracting nectar
from this earth
evolving flower,
translating
to blank page
my time here
in this body.

LIGHT NOW LIKE FEATHER

Fall's fire runs red across the hills
A memory runs through

me like a river
Cumberland

carving out a path
in this hallowed earth

calling out to me
you have returned

hawk-headed feral warrior
earth child, panther-bird

light now like feather
the long lashes of the sun

with a caress and a whisper
welcome to your temple

MITAKUYE OYASIN

> Lakota phrase meaning *all are related/all my relations*

I make my way
a joyous escape
to the jagged cliff-crowned
doorway to the mountains.

Here water shapes
every surface
with a wavy
swirling motion

like fingerprints left
by a great ancient ocean.
Each rock face bears
these marine tattoos.

Here, no longer
trapped on the treadmill
but another wild animal
in the congress of creatures.

Fondled by an under story
of a million ferns and trillium
as I follow a single narrow path
through wildflower woods.

Kissed by incessant
ticks and thirsty mosquitoes.
Dazzled by five-lined skinks
and cave salamanders.

Drawn to dainty flying dragons
and turtles painted orange.
Awed by a slew of cursive serpents

and a big blue sky surfed by red-tailed hawks.

I am cleansed in cool springs
thick with tiny frogs and cautious crawdads.
Baptized in thin creeks that seep
slow from earth's many hidden crevices.

Soaked with rain, rivers and lakes
and worn with the work of reclaiming
of walking this old land naming
all my neighbors, related.

BECOMING A MAN

A tiny village of six tents
bustles near the shore of a wide river.
The mountain is scary up above us,
darker than the woods. I sit quiet and uneasy,
clutching my favorite rock in my pocket,
hands snug in cotton gloves, but long underwear
and flannel no substitute for momma's hugs.
You're a big boy now, Scott. Old enough to go
camping without your mother there by your side;
her voice, a lullaby in my mind. Comforting
stars twinkle like street lights.
When I look up it is like looking down,
the night earth its own sky, speckled
with fires and lights. Trees taller than steeples
stand dark, silent guardians around the camp.
I think they could be monsters, big black beasts
twisting long arms out to snatch us from our fun.

A burst of laughter, the sizzle and crackle
of fire gathering strength draws me back
to the joy of boys. I watch my cousin, his friends,
too cool to speak to me, breaking twigs to feed
the flames while the others gather more logs
out where their bodies become the darkness.
I watch a spark dance up and away. Home
is not far, just down the road, below in the valley
by our church where Preacher Tom warns
of such wild dangers. And I know momma
is staring out the kitchen window wondering
if her little boy is learning something more
about becoming a man.

BECOMING VEGETARIAN

I.

My first trip
we followed papaw into the dark
of the farm's open fields,
carried piercing spears,
long forks for gigging frogs.
Our spotlight lit a circle
around a paralyzed mother,
a bloom of babies nearby,
a blur of eyes
looking back at us blinded.
Suddenly, my cousin stabbed
where light illumined water.
One quick jab—
the surface of the pond
no longer calm.

II.

I inherited
my role as fisherman
from both grandfathers,
addicted to the peace
of the shore
where the wait
for a catch
could take hours.
I'll never forget
one afternoon
by that big pond
right behind Purnell's

Old Folks, where live flesh is
manufactured. Sausage
and bacon. Hogs turned to ham,
shoulders and loins,
goooood.

Those poor pigs,
a soundtrack of death,
they just kept squealing.

III.

Chickens stacked
on the back of an 18 wheeler
in an open air cage
like holocaust survivors
gaunt and gray,
wind ripping what's left
of their feathers
from shivering bodies.
Their eyes! penetrating
shout such quiet terror.
I had to tear myself away
to the point of tears.

IV

"Wanna make
some extra money?"
my friend asked
over the phone
early one Saturday.

Broke as most
fifteen year olds,
I said, "yes."
Next stop,
Caudill's Flyers,
a place to place bets
then shoot skeet
or pigeons.
Our job
to gather the dead
each unlucky survivor.

A weathered and thin
farm hand named Julian
taught us with a live
demonstration how
boys became men.
You had to take them
by the head
and snap
their delicate necks.

The next eight hours
made eternity seem a blink.
When finally freed
from our agonizing task,
he took us back to town
in a beat up old Ford
to the safety of our homes;
the drive, cigarette smoke
and quiet, two boys
newly bruised beneath

another peeled layer.
The sun too tired
to hold itself up.

A NATIVE SPEAKS FROM THE GRAVE

You could confuse me
for a coyote at one hundred
yards or more
with a naked eye
or through a rifle's sight.

You could make the claim
you were clearing the property
boundary of predators,
an honest mistake
for a hunter or landowner.

You would find my body
much larger up close
where a single bullet
hole weeps fresh blood.

It would lead you
to question what it was
you chose to kill
that quiet afternoon
when the crows cawed summer
lazy with the chatter of cicada.

The authorities would come
to witness my cadaver
cold on a bed of blooming
Kentucky ground, would leave
with a tissue sample
to be sent to the lab for analysis.

They would tell you
of their suspicion—my lifeless
carcass closely resembled

a majestic wild animal, endangered
avatar of old Turtle Island wilderness.

They would confiscate my precious
salt and pepper pelt
when the DNA sample
revealed my suspected identity.

They would tell you I was *Canis lupus*
a gray wolf, the first confirmed
in Kentucky since the mid-eighteenth century.

They could not know
after nearly two hundred years
I was only trying to get back home.

FRACTURED APPALACHIA

Down home hound dog. Dixie
crème doughnut. Crackling
corn pone. Cackling coon porn.
Come on down the mountain
and come see our angels
over on car lot knob.
Trailer park graveyard. Full
gospel church. Half mountain view.

It's hard to stumble
when you're on your knees

on the billboard of Scalf Chapel
just off the main drag outside Bimble
where Old Dixie's bars and stars
are for sale under blue tarp tents
like laundry hung on the line to dry.
Lost causes still haunt like demons
won't die. Lost sons choke on rope
and that dope doctors prescribe.
Self-reliance commits slow suicide.
Crystals mined in abandoned trailers.
Vacant boxes by blacker roads. A blight
of drive thru nipples, sucked dry
to ghost town, downtown dwindles.
Dammed rivers slow to a trickle. Sand
won't bring a damn nickel.

Broke. Hear high lonesome notes
float circular where hawks soar,
this country's black and blues.
Cherokee on tear soaked trails.
No trace of buffalo, only ghosts

Natives tamed or slaughtered.
Earth plundered.
Settlers selling more
and more of themselves.
Locals peddle clothes
on the side of the road.

will haul
paint or hammer
for a few dollars
just holler

Chainsaws and bulldozers,
gargantuan machines and dynamite
bombs leave footprints and stumps,
eroded slopes, scraped flat
scarred back, a manmade disaster.
The only quilts seen from outer space,
swatches of disfigured mountain tops
like cancer devouring mother.
Buffet culture covers the land
of Tecumseh and Boone
like kudzu.

Crown bologna and American cheese.
A sign says
free hotdog drink prayer
In big letters, JESUS IS LORD
from the holy mountain proclaimed.
How long before it too is taken?

TVA and king coal tattoos. Too many
abandoned gardens. Old homesteads

falling into disrepair. A woman waters
her crops to fight what is drying up.
An old man fiddles to keep the spirit alive.
God save the mountains!

I saw four generations on a front porch.
When the fourth is old enough
they will leave home,
no looking back, fast on uneven lanes.
To the cities and beyond the plains
Searching for work.

Tension builds like goldenrod
blooms in September, all over
Appalachia. This land
where the hearts of women
and the backs of men are broken
beneath an incalculable industrial burden.

THE WATCHMAN

Like the purple finch
singing into the crash-bang
city that always moans
you can find me high
above the roar
on a watchman's branch
melancholic at the end
of the day
yearning beautifully.

OLD FRANKFORT PIKE IS A SPINE OF MINE

1.

Clash at the edge of scenic corridors
What is called progress is an insatiable force
Threatens to move us in reverse

We make the choice
What to preserve, what to destroy
Keep driving into the storm

I slow down
Enough to see

Herds of whitetail crossing savannahs forgotten
Undulating pastures haunted by dead giants
Rich remnants ruled by chinquapin and bur

2.

The Elkhorn holds a secret—

I am Pegasus
Racing against darkness
My demise, sprinting down
Limestone-walled back stretches
Awakened now as the afternoon dies

Foals nap near their mare mothers
Dream or déjà vu?
Again I am the hero
Confined to the haphazard
Sprawl of civilization

I scrawl salvation
Strategy into the infinity
Of an empty page

3.

Our state house of weapons looks on
Promises there will always be
Bullets. Captives. Victors. I capture
Its image from the shadows

Few remember
The dead
Atop the palisade around the bend
Tombs and monuments crown
The capitol, its golden dome
Glimmers in gray dusk

It's the idea that watches over us

4.

Trees know no night
Where leaders are
Supposed to lead, the lanterns
On the bridge are dim

One wooly mullein makes a home
In a crack in a forgotten wall
Does not care
Who calls charge!

I neigh this night song beside a rising river

O, sycamores! Standing here witness
More majestic than those towers
More commanding than this Capitol
Tell brother-sister box elder, red cedar
To inherit the future with you

I fear we are too
Hungry for blood, too
Reliant on war, too committed to
Ignorance to join you

SURVIVAL MECHANISM

Oh ominous megalopolis,
millennial crowds encased in black
cloaks. Rerun of five o'clock
funeral procession, awful impatience at the end
of the workday. Unbelievable individual
detachment, survival mechanism activated.

I am not afraid,
just claustrophobic.
People like a pulsation in every direction,
trains coming and going,
a consistent rumble beneath the streets.
Earthworms work earth somewhere I'm sure.

Tongues twisted with accents,
seldom seen smiles but sad masks,
the prospect of terror in suspicious glances.
All colors of strangers stacked
shoulder to shoulder in seats made of plastic.

Their noses in books and newspapers.
Ears plugged with headphones.
Staring at cell phones or eyes closed.
Some playing possum, some try and sleep.
I sit with a quiet smile
knowing my visit will soon come to an end.

LIFEBOAT

I can see
you need
a lifeboat
a set of strong
arms wrapped
around you
one brave hand
reaching up
from the abyss
but my previous
rescue attempts
have ended
in failure.

I was a lifeguard
who instinctively
dove in
battled the waves
and changing currents
to save another
only to find
that I had
forgotten
how to swim.

Someone
had to drown
so I let go.

I did
everything I
possibly could
to get back

to the safety
of the shore
but I
cannot lie.

It was a pathetic
dog paddle;
I could not help
but swallow
salty water.

And now
having reached
the beach
having lost
so much before
to the awful bottom
I cannot even
stand to stick
one little toe
into any body
of water.

THE TIDE

licking your back
as you lay face down
finally forced to confirm
the earth beneath you
knows you are
no different
than any other
grain of sand it washes
over, wears away.

KENTUCKY IS MY BODY

I am a graveyard
a farm converting crops
to cement
a barn who lost the gift of tobacco
still stained with its scent

my aroma: sour mash
coal burning power plants
wildflower blooms and natural gas
redbuds, magnolias

I am cigarette smoke and cancer
strip malls like sunspots on a burned back
another and another
and another
church
acres and acres churned up
in the worship of money

Kentucky
is
my body

I am sweet water
sinking through skin to limestone
bone, a circulatory system
pushing blood through veins
beyond dams and stints
clots of plaque, cans and plastic

I am black lungs
bellowing the song my granny
sung over a hot stove while mashing
potatoes pulled from garden ground

before any future conversion
to cul-de-sac

I am a crooked spine
of knobs and mountaintops
centered only by serpentine
sway of back roads, my soul
where front porch stories
still echo

Kentucky
is
my body

and I am a gun rack
locked in a spare bedroom
where quilts lay spread
across peaceful beds

RECLAMATION

The dragonflies appear
to be doing fine,
dance about my work
as if there were no such thing.

Wind sings when
meeting tree limbs.

Peeper and *Terrapene*
join the black king for a sip
where spring leaks
into a tiny pool.

I join them
in reflection.

The long hours labored
having dug with hands and shovel,
wrestled rocks and clumps,
hauled wheelbarrows and buckets
to reclaim myself,

the head of the spring, the beauty
and balance in existence before
bulldozers came to scrape
the treasure chest clean.
Left the land wounded to weep.

My work stretched out by the sun
slowly sailing across the sky.
I raise both arms up and breathe.
A spider's web connects two trees.
The black king orbits me like a moon.

This is our home.
My day has been a slow journey
of healing all along the switch-
backs of the mind.

I am the snake
winding from one
end of the wetland
to the other.

TURTLE SLOW

on recuperating logging road
pale jewelweed and Joe-Pye shimmy

Indian pipe like tobacco pipes
gray-white against ten shades
of green gorge slopes

fingers of fungus jump up
from moist sandstone
boulder shadows

poplar, beech, oak fabric
a forest quilt
feel humming life pulse
everywhere beneath sky

by god
there is no god
but this voluptuous goddess

a great mother
tending the needs
of her many children

springs, creeks, rivers
when I need water

fruit, nut, flesh
when I need sustenance

cave, canopy, cliff
when I need shelter

pet, kin, companion
when I need love

CONE OF JUVENILITY

      is the tendency of young trees to hold onto dead leaves within their centers; is a mechanism to aid in survival. It is within this cone-shaped area that new sprouts will develop and grow in order to replace branches lost or damaged.

Hold on
to the tender
leaves rustling
on the branches
of your delicate heart.
Hold on to them
as long as you
are able.

MICROCOSM

creek beds
are cradled in
the creases of
maple leaves

HOW TO RESTORE A FOREST

cordon off
area to be restored

visually
or physically

do not
cut one thing

inside
the boundary

BIOMIMICRY

Pay attention.

You might disturb
a monarch in an open field
perched on a milkweed stem,
a sharp-shinned zeroing in
on rodent din-din,
or a great blue heron
fishing almost invisible
along the rocky bend
of a secret creek.

Pay attention to every step.
The universe might blink.

RELIGIOSA*

Shards of sun
Flit across a continent
In and out
Of our imagination
Aztec-Olmec-Maya heart

Destination—a forest of sacred fir
High altitude hibernation
Shimmering winter miracle
Oyamel's orange body
Crown to root, a sheath of small wings

* *Abies religiosa*: sacred fir, native to central and southern Mexico, western Guatemala (known as Oyamel in Spanish)

SUNS AND MOONS

> "Nature hates calculators."
> —Ralph Waldo Emerson

Weaving in
and out, a fractal
tight Kentucky nooks
I travel

this path through
paradise and marvel
at roadside bazaars
cluttered with junk.

Two men lean
into an open hood
the jaw of a beaten
down clunker.

A dirty
dog with muddy
paws bites air
instead of butterfly

floating
down
to
cool water.

No road reaches
the river bank
only this trail
blazed by rough bucks
and svelte does.

Statuesque sycamores
tower, stand guard
watching over
the holy Licking.

It reminds me
quieter than a tree
full of crows yap
to be still, listen.

So much is said
without a mouth.
All of our senses
are like ears.

Earth spins
its tune
in an imperfect
circle.

Time counts
no numbers
but suns
and moons.

OFF THE WAGON OUTSIDE WADDY

I still think about the moon
seeping in through the barn
slats while we sat splintered
on warped wagon planks
under rafters hung heavy
with harvest tobacco;
the faraway forest ringing
hilltop pasture an apparition
shrouded by dew.

SAVIOR

Moon is my savior tonight
a sliver smiling silver
through the living room window

urging me to grin
or laugh like a hyena
even though I feel like crying.

It has appeared there
just in the last hour
perfectly in the corner of my eye

when pain pierces
my heart sharp and spasms
quake in my back.

It falls quietly toward earth,
across my mind
toward the farthest side of the world.

SPIDERS

understand
the importance of light.
Watch them weave delicate webs
near the burning epicenter
then wait patiently
for flies and moths
to arrive.

THE CENTER

  the
Light
gleams
 like
a serpent
illuminating
 the darkened
   ground
  seeking
the center
of all living
    t
     h
      i
     n
    g
     s

GOOD MUD

In the damp-dark don't
you just want to fall
into it all—
feather, leaf, creek
good mud?

ALLEGIANCE

> Inspired by Warren Byrom's song *Get Real (After the Storm)*

I pledge allegiance
To the dirt
Beneath my feet
Wherever I happen to stand

And to this planet
For which it is a crucial part

One rainbow of a species
Under the sparkle of cosmos
Indistinguishable to any earthworm
Practicing peace and justice
For all y'all

MUDROOM CATHARSIS

Swing the hammer swift
and demolish the rotten.
Earwigs and termites creep.
Suddenly an opening,
the space where spider
and snake thrive.
A shaded face that can finally
feel the breeze.

Send away the ants!
Remove the carcass of a cat.
Pull away bent doors
and sledge all the crumbling walls.
Root out the cracked foundation
and gently pick up broken glass.
Rebuild something beautiful.
But first,

let in light.

INSTRUCTIONS

Get out of your car
and grab a bus or bicycle.

Buy fewer things, closer to home.

Abandon chemicals
and shun all forms of poison.

Bless your body
and grow
a garden.

Use electricity sparingly.

Light candles
and let the mind entertain.

Water is most sacred
flowing through the universe
of you. It is
the blood of the world.

Protect it
as you would
your heart, your children.

And love with an abundance
that illumines and lightens.

Everything you
can touch or trample
is precious and connected.

NEW FIRE

An arrow of geese
across the sky.
Time of new fire.
A nail in the cross
of my conviction.

It will take many more
than me to free us
from the cage of old fires
now cold coals
atop a world of ash.

There is nothing left
to burn but the past.
The old way
will not keep us
warm anymore.

GREAT SPIRIT APPRENTICE

I am slowly learning
the language of land.
It may take a life-
time or more
to advance my education.
But at least when I pass
over to the realm
of singing light
I will cross over
knowing the whole
time I was engaged
in conversation with god.

NOTHING LASTS FOREVER

Surely a moon rules
over all this beauty
and mess, yes?
Feel the tug of a full one
just before sun sets
on another kaleidoscopic
Kentucky afternoon.
Threshold upon threshold
we cross. Hand in hand
or severed, but together.
Nothing lasts forever.
Just ask a mother
a lover
or a mountain.

RUIN

is a message embedded
in crude maps, the schizophrenia
of cities, disorder of colonies,
civilizations chicken scratched in dirt,
cursive highways of borers
like Braille beneath bark,
stick figure caricatures for future diggers
who unearth the evidence left, black coals in a pit.

They say this isn't the bottom,
graveyard of bedrock, but the bone
of an all-knowing being
cracking beneath the crunch of steely centuries.
Every crevice opened
overturns the new order of dust,
gilded towers devoured by rust, the contours
of a Great Face erode, a memory is lost.

DISAPPEAR

Sweeping the dead
June bugs off the porch
cicadas click their tymbals
from every surrounding canopy.

There is a poster
of all types of butterflies
leaning against brick
a relic of apartment walls
destined for the cabin in Menifee
—swallowtail, fritillary, monarch—

A co-worker says he hasn't seen
one monarch this year (me neither)
their population fallen
by a staggering ninety percent.

The seasons keep racing
and the dust accumulates
on the porch. Like a good
human, I sweep until clean
every week, fighting what I know
deep down is inevitable.

The *Magicicada* spends
most of their lives underground
thirteen or seventeen years.
Into what kind of world
will they emerge next time?

What magnificent creatures
lost forever?

This is ink. This is paper.
It too will disappear.

EARTH IS MY CHURCH

"Conviction is worthless unless it is converted into conduct"
—Thomas Carlyle

Where Cherokee,
Adena, and Shawnee paused
on altars of limestone, under
arches of sandstone, at home
in their own Eden,
there is a place of singing
energy. More than rock
and soil, it is my center.

Sky alive
with buzzard and hawk.
Wind and cloud lit by golden
sun, the spirit spark,
shines through stained
glass branches of hemlock,
beech and oak, my thoughts.

In a holler carved by millennia
of rainstorms and relentless
meandering rivers, I meditate
where whippoorwill and woodpecker
shout the sun and moon down. Hallelujah!

Earth is my church.

Though wicked forces spit hymns
of venom from the tips of forked
tongues. Their fangs, the tools
of industry, thirst for every
drop of blood from the body,

my temple. Spirit nearly extinct.
Vital signs plummet like empires
decline and death for profit
appears the gospel
good people have been
fooled into believing.

It is not enough to hide
away with faith, resign to prayer.
One must act to trigger
true transformation.

Go! Take to the sanctity
and abundance of the wilderness
wherever you can find it. Wildness
resides in even the smallest spaces.
Seek consistent communion with your god.
Self-sufficiency, the real revelation.

PINE MOUNTAIN: A WORK IN PROGRESS

Morning is hawk shriek
Stretching our bones toward heaven
The fog-drenched ridge line

Caravan along the snake
Of highway splitting Pine and
Black is wrecked by coal
A mirror of Appalachian alternatives
Revelation on the airwaves
Which side are you on, which side are you on?

We choose to turn into wilderness
Away from destruction
Toward Bad Branch, above the falls

It begins with a bear
Paw, fresh pressed
Into a mud puddle
Ursus americanus
Our collective drawn
Into a circle

Welcome to Pine Mountain
Crucial east coast wildlands corridor
One hundred and twenty-five mile
Back bone

The danger is not in losing
Our lives in an attack by bear
But in failure to protect
The wildest places that sustain us
The headwaters, the forests, the mountains

Along the path
Every detail is a wormhole
Amphibians slither at our feet
Lichens filter the air entering lungs
Like humans we chat
Poke and examine scat
Another sign we are not alone
The hemlock is not
The only one endangered here

We enter a timber cathedral
Mixed mesophytic, all light
Siphoned into the narrow valley
Through a stained glass canopy
Tones color us with rainbows

Suddenly a wind
Descending silences the pack
A murmuration of leaves
Rains down like autumn confetti
There are moments you know
You are connected
To god, the creator
Whatever you name the sacred

This is it
The moment of communion
We breathe it into our bodies
Stand quiet in the silent language of the holy
The earth church
Lose ourselves in its glory

Emergent from the shaded gorge
Of our centering we ascend
Toward High Rock
Stepping out of the womb
Onto the back of the mountain
Fully bathed in midday sun
The slant of the megalithic outcrop
Leans toward the sky

Our slow procession becomes a sprint
Toward the summit
Fueled by the childish joy
You always feel when you are
On the verge of discovering
Something new

So quiet here
You forget
The city

A few small ones scattered on the horizon
Remind us of our mission, to reach the people

Returning from our high place inspired
There is no such wonder at the gas station
Didn't take long to return to the conflict
One sick sight is the shot piercing the stomach

A black corpse fills the bed of a pickup
Ursus americanus

The way we treat the land is a reflection
Of the way we treat each other

I write this with a gut tangled with worry
Art is the oath of action we have taken
At the end of the day, hope is the intoxicant

Perhaps one day, in reflection on all our good work
We will find reassurance that it made a difference

Another generation will be able
To sit under old growth
And sing songs by fire light
The wilderness preserved and alive
Everywhere, just outside the boundary of skin

ABOUT THE AUTHOR

Pushcart Prize nominee, Poet Laureate of Al's Bar, and creative force behind Holler Poets Series, Eric Scott Sutherland is an ISA certified arborist, a member of the Pine Mountain Collective, Urban Forest Initiative, and founding board member of Kentucky Writers and Artists for Reforestation (KWAR). *Earth Is My Church* is his fifth book of poetry. A native Kentuckian, he makes his home with his wife, son, and menagerie of family pets in the heart of Lexington, Kentucky.

ACKNOWLEDGMENTS

The author would like to thank the editors of these magazines and journals, and the organizers of the projects where the following poems first appeared:

Kentucky Is My Body, *Pine Mountain Sand & Gravel* #14, 2011

Light Now Like Feather, *Artscene* #13, Winter 2010

Gorge, *Artscene* #13, Winter 2010

Turtle Slow, *Artscene* #13, Winter 2010

Earth Evolving Flower, *Artscene* #13, Winter 2010

Mitakuye Oyasin (as Sacred Relations), *Artscene* #13 and online in *Public Republic*, 2010

Proof, *Artscene* #13 and online in *Public Republic*, 2010

Microcosm, *Bigger Than They Appear: Anthology of Very Short Poems*, Accents Publishing, 2011

Off The Wagon Outside Waddy, anthology/multi-media project *Pet Milk*, 2009

New Fire, *The Single Hound*, Issue #1, 2011

Earth Is My Church, *The Single Hound*, Issue #3, Special Kentucky Edition, 2011

Becoming A Man, finalist, *Still the Journal*'s annual poetry competition, 2012; *Still the Journal* #12, Summer, 2013

Nothing Lasts Forever, *Pine Mountain Sand & Gravel* #16, 2013

Ruin, included in artist Laurie Doctor's exhibit anthology, *Another Night in the Ruins*, 2014

Disappear, *Kudzu*, Spring, 2014

Old Frankfort Pike Is a Spine of Mine, *The Good Gray Project*, a civic art project, 2015

Reclamation, *Full: An Anthology of Moon Poems*, Two of Cups Press, 2016

Pine Mountain: A Work in Progress, *Pine Mountain Collective*, a group project, 2016; *Pine Mountain Sessions*, CD/LP audio recording, 2019